Also by Louis Jenkins

Tin Flag

Before You Know It, Prose Poems 1970-2005

European Shoes

North of the Cities

*In the Sun
Out of the Wind*

*In the Sun
Out of the Wind*

Prose Poems by

Louis Jenkins

Will o' the Wisp Books

Copyright © 2017 by Louis Jenkins

All rights reserved. Except for brief quotations in critical articles or reviews, no part of this book may be reproduced in any manner without prior written permission from the author: willothewispbooks.com

Published by Will o' the Wisp Books 2017

Printed in Minneapolis, MN

Cover illustration by Rick Allen
Cover design by Amy Jenkins & Marc Iwanin

ISBN 978-0-9793128-7-8

Will o' the Wisp Books
Bloomington, Minnesota
willothewispbooks.com

"Sitting quietly, doing nothing
Spring comes, and the
grass grows, by itself."

Matsuo Basho

Table of Contents

Black Bears | 13

Why? | 14

A Clearing | 15

Unfortunate Location | 16

October | 17

The Woods in Fall | 18

Day's Catch | 19

After Midnight | 20

Restoration | 21

Winter Clothes | 22

Spring Wind | 23

Crows Behind the House | 24

Ducks | 25

Untroubled | 26

Here and There | 27

Smile | 28

North Shore | 29

Deep Blue Sea | 30

Beautiful Women | 31

Putty from Vaseline | 32

Waiting | 33

West Wind | 34

The Dreamtime | 35

Blue Shirt | 36

Lucky | 37

Inheritance | 38

Ships | 39

Going through a Phase | 40

Leoti | 41

Heritage | 42

Smoking | 43

The Painter | 44

From the Train | 45

First Day of School | 46

The Learning Curve | 47

Spring Again | 48

As Is | 49

Supervisor | 50

A Man Builds a House | 51

Ineffable | 52

Could | 53

The Black Journal | 54

As the Light Turns Green | 55

Saints | 56

Nothing in Particular | 57

Worldly Goods | 58

Complete Strangers | 59

What We Mean When We Say It's a Beautiful Day | 60

Fidget | 61

Soup | 62

Small Things | 63

Hidden Meanings | 64

Yellow Hat | 65

Black Bears

I like black bears. They are relatively common around here, and they are usually not aggressive. Actually, they are generally affable, loners mostly, but not opposed to hanging out with humans now and then. In fact, I've found that in many ways they are a lot like us.

My friend, Richard, an older male, drops by now and then and we hang out down on the shore, have a couple of beers, but mostly we just sit and look out at the water. We don't have a lot to say. We aren't friends exactly, but we enjoy the company. Richard says, at our age we don't have friends. We have associates.

Why?

I ask myself. Because when you finally need to go home this is the only place to go to. And when you get there there's nothing; just the blank page. Well, maybe there's a patch of dry bare ground, underneath an old cottonwood tree, a bit of sun, a crow in the next field. You can add things or take them away. Youth was the age of acquisition. Now you find that there aren't many things you need, but the garage and the attic are still full. I'm OK with the dirt and the cottonwood tree. It's not the bodhi tree, but my expectations are not high. The oceans are deep and dark and the briny water goes on for thousands of miles, but you only need a cupful or so to drown in.

A Clearing

There is something about a clearing that makes me feel uneasy, something too sunny and optimistic about this break in the constant shade, those nervous poplars and gloomy spruce all turned to face an open space as if they expected something to happen here: the blank page on which something should be written.

Paavo Wirkkila got an idea, cleared the land and grew hay. Nothing else grows very well around here. He kept a horse to help with the hay then fed the hay to the horse. A limited plan. When the old man died he left the buildings to fall, left the clearing to the county and sapling popple trees. He also left this heap of stones he'd cleared from the field, not a monument, no part of his plan, just an annoyance he tried to push out of his earthly way.

Unfortunate Location

In the front yard there are three big white pines, older than anything in the neighborhood except the stones. Magnificent trees that toss their heads in the wind like the spirited black horses of a troika. It's hard to know what to do, tall dark trees on the south side of the house, an unfortunate location, blocking the winter sun. Dark and damp. Moss grows on the roof, the porch timbers rot and surely the roots have reached the old bluestone foundation. At night, in the wind, a tree could stumble and fall, killing us in our beds. The needles fall year after year making an acid soil where no grass grows. We rake the fallen debris, nothing to be done. We stand around with sticks in our hands. Wonderful trees!

October (above Lake Superior)

A north wind shakes the last few yellow leaves clinging to a thin popple tree. It's easy to tell what's coming. Old leaves must fall to make way for the new. That's all well and good as long as it's not your turn to go. Keep the dead waiting! Keep the unborn waiting! There's not much to this life anyway, some notions, some longings that come and go like the sea, like sun and shadow played across the stone. This weather is not so bad if you can find a place among the rocks in the sun and out of the wind.

The Woods in Fall

In the city it seems no one treats you as a human being. The woods, on the other hand, are full of things that do, that run if you come too close. It's lonely. Who will I talk to? Who will I invite to my birthday party? Bears tend to overindulge and fall asleep. Alfred, the great gray owl, commonly known as Al Owl, can never remember anyone's name…. The days are bright and the nights clear and cold. Most all the leaves have fallen by now, the red and orange maple, the yellow birch and poplar. Only the somber evergreens are unmoved. If I clear a few of the dead leaves from this little pool there is the perfect sky again, on the other side, and a face, not quite mine, but that apes my every move and refuses to go away until I do.

Day's Catch

I usually bring a few fish home every evening. After I've cleaned them I always leave one fish out on the stump beside the shed. In the morning the fish is gone. I don't know what takes it, if it's a weasel or a raccoon or a bear. I don't watch, or try to track whatever it is. I put the fish out in the evening at suppertime, and in the morning it's gone.

After Midnight

After midnight Woodland Avenue is quiet for the most part, an occasional car and then a motorcycle winding up, going way too fast. Someone drunk with love or the lack thereof, drunk with speed, with despair or joie de vivre, someone young and immortal, stalking death. "Live fast, love hard, die young and leave a beautiful memory." But memory is short, not much more than the day after tomorrow. So go ahead then I say, take some innocent bystanders with you—passion is over in an eyeblink, whether you die or live.

Restoration

The idea was to restore one of these Victorian monsters to its original grandeur--with a modern kitchen and bathroom, of course, and it would need a new furnace. We'd have to do most of the work ourselves but low-cost home improvement loans were available.

In the old days things were built to last.... giant oak timbers imbedded in granite, cast iron cogwheels and worm gears that drove certain adjuncts of the heavenly spheres. Pieces remain but no one remembers exactly what they were for.

In those days fuel was cheap. One could heat several rooms with an afternoon's discussion on the subject of free will. Inside one of the cupboards is a special small door to the outside, like a pet door, so the cold could come in.

With rotten timbers, plaster falling all around, this job requires a will of iron, like the border fence, bent and rusted near the ground, that still hangs on like God and empire. We'd paint this place in true colors of the period, dark green and red, repression and madness.

Winter Clothes

We come in puffing and stamping-- goose down, wool, heavy boots, mittens, scarf.... Winter clothes bear the same relationship to the body as the body does to the soul, a sort of cocoon where those you thought you knew are changed beyond recognition. .... We greet each other with awkward affection, like bears. Someone removes a glove and extends a pale hand.

His hand on the green silk of her dress, lightly, on the small of her back, sleepwalking there in the forest. And on the inside, the raveled thread ends, untidy windfall where the hunter walks to flush the startled bird. . . and afterwards silence, a handful of feathers, like letters from another woman found in a bank box after his death, casting a whole new light on the subject.

The mind insists that we live on after death whether we walk stiffly in bodies cold and drained of color or drift like tall columns of mist across the northern lakes, taller than we were in life but no more substantial.

We must look inside to find the answer, pulling the layers away like the leaves of an artichoke. And the answer is incorrect.

Spring Wind

The spring wind comes through and knocks over trashcans and trees. It has something to do with warm fronts and cold fronts, I think, or with high and low pressure systems, things that I don't really understand and that aren't really an explanation anyway. Ultimately the spring wind is the result of some relationship between the earth and the sun that may not be all that healthy, after all. The wind comes in a big huff, slams doors, pushes things around and kicks up the dirt. The big bully spring wind comes through on its way nowhere and, ha ha! We love it.

Crows Behind the House

Crows have gathered in the trees behind the house, cawing and carrying on all afternoon. They are upset about something. We have been told how smart crows are, how they can recognize individual human faces, how they can learn to use tools, how they can communicate. Which is great, except that they hardly ever shut up. Crows are very intelligent, perhaps as smart or smarter than monkeys or chimpanzees, which to my mind, given their ubiquity, puts them in strong contention for second most annoying species on the planet. Or maybe third, behind mosquitoes.

Ducks

There are two types of ducks, divers and dabblers. Divers feed on fish, plants and insects in deep water. They live on big lakes and rivers. Dabblers prefer shallow water, ponds and creeks where they feed on plants and insects. Dabblers are also known as puddle ducks. Once, on a very rainy day, I saw a mallard land on water that had accumulated in the street, not more than 6 or 7 inches deep. If I decided to be a duck I'd probably choose to be a dabbler, it's more my nature, dabbling here and there, farting around, not like a diver, some sharp-billed merganser intent on something lurking in the deep. And unlike the diving ducks who need a long runway to become airborne, running and flapping along the surface of the water, dabblers take off from the water with a sudden, upward leap into the air.

Untroubled

One wearies of matters of substance, those weighty matters that one feels should be resolved, the dilemma of life on earth, the existence of extraterrestrial life, the existence of God. Instead I recommend those moments that, seemingly without reason, stay with you for a lifetime: that red-haired girl on the shore brushing her teeth as we sailed away; the glimpse of a face; a bare shoulder turning in a doorway; moments like music, beauty and truth untroubled by meaning.

Here and There

Some days I don't know if I'm coming or going, as they say. Don't know if I'm here or there. I am here and you are there. Except, of course, when you are here or I am there. I much prefer it when you are here. Then it seems that spring is truly on the way, that the sun is warming and the lilacs will bloom. But then sometimes I think that you are not really here, that there is a faraway look in your eyes, that in fact you are far away. I don't know where you are, London? New York? Maybe you are just outside the door, but you are there and I am still here.

Smile

There is a beautiful young woman behind the counter and for no apparent reason she gives me a smile that is devastating. It is a smile that is like the sunlight coming through the heavy clouds and turning the surface of the water all glittery silver. It is a smile that says anything is possible, that I am the one she has been waiting for, that I am 25 again. I think she must be the most cruel person on the planet. She puts her hand under mine as she gives me my change, and all I can say is "Oh my heart."

North Shore

On a clear day like today I can see the Wisconsin shore all the way to Outer Island and miles of white-capped waves rising and falling between here and there. The rock I am sitting on is huge and round with a fringe of moss, like hair, around the edge just below the waterline. It is like sitting atop a monk's head. I reach down and the cold water surges up to touch my hand. It occurs to me that we are already under weigh and I have no idea how to pilot this thing.

Deep Blue Sea

Everyday I write in my notebook, at work on my book of poems that I will dedicate to you, even though you have gone away. I write, "Today the sea is as blue as your eyes." Or "The sea is not as blue as your eyes" Or "The sea is more blue than your eyes." Or "I am more blue than the sea, or than you, who are not blue at all except for your eyes".... The writing does not go well.

Beautiful Women

There are all these women, beautiful young women and they circle around you, no, not circle but they pass so close. They have things to do, places to go, they stride past you on the street in their skirts and high boots and you want to say wait, wait…and one gives you a quick kiss as she passes by and you want to say wait…but there is another…and then they are all gone…and they pass far away, like objects in the sky, like a satellite, like some blinking billionaire's jet plane, silent, high above, and down here on earth it's turning cold and it's late.

Putty from Vaseline

Did I tell you about the newlyweds who could not tell putty from Vaseline? Yes, my wife says, about 100 times. That's the trouble, I say, you know every one of my stories and jokes, I need a new young woman to tell my stories to. You could try getting some new stories, my wife says. No, that's no good. I'm too old for that, all that stuff happened when I was young. What I need is a fresh ear, a beautiful young woman who would laugh and think that maybe my stories were even profound and she'd hug me and say, Let's go for a ski, and then go out dancing. And I'd say, Can't we just stay in this afternoon, make a fire…? Then she'd say, Come on, don't be an old fuddy-duddy. If you don't want to come along I'll go alone. Wait, I'd say. Did I tell you about the newlyweds…?

Waiting

Years I spent waiting for you to come to me here on this shore, rehearsing what we would say to one another and thinking of the happiness that would be ours. Now that I am old it occurs to me that you must have come, but I was too distracted to see you there.

West Wind

It isn't so much because of the desire for what has been lost, as it is the loss of desire itself, that I stand here, like a child whose big rubber ball has washed out to sea, on the verge of tears, becoming aware that there is no possibility of return.

The Dreamtime

Those were the days of beer and deep-fried chicken livers, at night we swam the laughing sea. You were so beautiful. It was still the dreamtime, we were still in the aureole of childhood that extended 100,000 light years into deep space. But eventually even that ended and we fell into our separate realities. Everything fell apart. We all went crazy, they discovered water on Mars, the Nasdaq went down 3 percent, and suddenly we were too old. Yet it would be great to meet you at the Dreamtime Supper Club for one last dance, and a cocktail, perhaps.

Blue Shirt

I've gotten up many a morning in recent years, taken a look in the mirror and said, "Alright, it's got to be the life of the mind from here on out." But despite tremendous effort I found myself incapable of a single thought, and totally exhausted by 10:00 AM. So looking good is important. Though in my case there is not much to work with, especially when I consider the ordinary mess of my life, the ragtag collection of mistakes and wrong turns, the worn out socks and underwear stored in a cardboard box. But I do have the blue shirt my wife bought for me. It is a beautiful dark blue, cut so that it hangs just right and made of a material that is comfortable in all seasons. Even though it doesn't make up for anything, and no one ever notices, I always feel good when I wear it.

Lucky

All my life I've been lucky. Not that I made money, or had a beautiful house or cars. But lucky to have had good friends, a wife who loves me, and a good son. Lucky that war and famine or disease did not come to my doorstep. Lucky that all the wrong turns I made, even if they did turn out well, at least were not complete disasters. I still have some of my original teeth. All that could change, I know, in the wink of an eye. And what an eye it is, bright blue contrasting with her dark skin and black hair. And oh, what long eyelashes! She turns and with a slight smile gives me a long slow wink, a wink that says, "Come on over here, you lucky boy."

Inheritence

My father came from nowhere in particular, and he was only distantly related to anyone, second cousin once removed. He came wearing a white suit, slammed into the hog pen when the brakes failed. The only things he owned were a few tools. He rose early. He went up and down the ladder, painting maroon or chartreuse, round and round the room in a sort of dance. He painted his face in a random pattern. Round and round till he fell down flat. I don't own the tools but I know some of the steps, some of the words to the song.

.

Ships

Many of my friends, now that their divorces are final and their children are grown up and have lives of their own, have moved into smaller shells somewhere up the shore. As for me, I still enjoy being all at sea, an intimate of the luminous life of the deep, bobbing up and down among ships that pass in the night, keeping my head just above water. But I don't worry, I know I'll get back to sleep when the morning fog comes in, when the Pacific fleet arrives, ghost ships from the Coral Sea. They come in silently and never cough or shuffle their feet but I know they're in the room, great hulking shapes, old and unpleasant relatives, the color of the sea, the color of the sky, gathered around my bed.

Going Through a Phase

My granddaughter, age two, lies on the floor and kicks and screams and cries, Mommy, Daddy! I need help! she sobs. It is a moment of existential angst. I know exactly what she means. She's going through a phase, they say. That's how life is, one phase after another. I remember the phase of thinking I was Elvis, even though I couldn't sing. And in junior high there was the phase of being "mentally challenged." I hung out all summer with the dumbest kid in school. We rode our bicycles aimlessly around town and one day on a quiet street I rode straight into the back of a parked car. Probably because of that incident, I have never fully recovered from that phase. In fact, in recent years I've detected a resurgence of the condition.

Leoti

Great Grandpa Charlie thought he could get rich in America so he came to Leoti, Kansas in the 1870s. There was a fight going on over which town, Leoti or nearby Coronado, would be the county seat. Wyatt Earp and Bat Masterson came to help shoot it out. Everybody felt there was money to be made. At this time, also, they were killing off the buffalo. Charlie got a wagon and gathered the bones of slaughtered buffalo to sell to be made into fertilizer, and the horns were made into buttons. By the time the bones were all gone he'd made enough to buy some land, get married and build a sod house. Great Grandpa didn't stay too many years. It was a difficult place to farm, flat and hard as a gaming table, treeless and dusty. Leoti won the war and is still county seat and the only town in the county. After the fight everyone moved out of Coronado. At the courthouse we located Great Grandpa's settlement on the big county map. My wife said, "We could drive out there and have a picnic." The clerk said, "I wouldn't do that if I were you. They raise a lot of pigs out there nowadays."

Heritage

Great-Grandmother Murphy was a proud woman. She came from a well-to-do family that had connections back east. She had presence and bearing. Great-Grandpa Murphy was an Irishman of dubious ancestry and background. Nevertheless they got married, as people do. Grandpa Murphy shuffled along as they walked downtown, looking at the ground or his feet. He found things that way; an Indian arrowhead, sometimes a nickel or a dime. A dime was worth something in those days. And here is a perfectly good comb, just needs to be boiled a bit to kill the bugs. Grandmother kept her head high as she walked along; she was a Smith, after all, one of *the* Smiths. But she never found anything.

Smoking

Back when I was a kid everyone smoked. My Grandpa smoked cigars, King Edwards. He'd buy them by the box. When the box was empty he'd give me the box. He chewed tobacco as well, Days Work, and he spit into the box of sawdust underneath the table saw. If he'd had the patch and the gum he probably would have done that too. For my dad, it was Lucky Strikes, but he never really had any luck. Uncle Rex, cigars, I think. Uncle Gerald, Old Gold, or maybe it was Chesterfields. Great Uncle Harve smoked a pipe. You'd see him driving down the road in his Ford coupe. He could barely see over the wheel, a short guy, but he smoked a big pipe. He lived into his 90s. While he was in the home, my mother would visit him and try to make him quit smoking. "I can see the burn holes in your pants from that filthy pipe." Uncle Harve took to coloring his leg through each hole with a marking pen so my mother wouldn't notice.

The Painter

After he has covered the earth the painter is ready to start on the sky. Beauty requires constant attention and, anyway, it's a living. What color is the sky today? Blue. He stirs the paint, pours half into his bucket and starts up the ladder one step at a time, slowly. He climbs above the trees, above the cows grazing in the field, above the rivers and mountains. He leans to one side and spits–a long way down. He doesn't like it much. He hooks his bucket to the ladder and dips his brush. He makes the first even stroke.

From the train

It was the backyard of some little house in a poor neighborhood at the edge of the city. The lawn was green and seemed well cared for, even though the yard was right next to the main track. Then I noticed two people in the yard, a man and a woman (of course) and they seemed at first to be wrestling, crouched facing each other and their hands gripping either each other's or some object. Or was it a child? Were they angry or was this just a playful moment? Were they struggling with some home-improvement project, trying to move a recalcitrant cement St. Francis? I couldn't really see and we passed so quickly. In only moments we were passing some small factories and sidetracks where there were what seemed like acres of rusting railway car wheels.

First Day of School

Goldenrod and tansy are blooming in the ditches, a few of the maple trees are beginning to turn, patches of red here and there among the green, blue sunny skies and white puffy clouds, but the air is cooler today. September. Day after tomorrow is the first day of school. New tennis shoes perhaps, some new pencils and a Big Chief tablet from Vaters' and if there is change back penny candy or a licorice flavored wax mustache. Some of the girls will have new dresses. There is an excitement in the air that will be short-lived. Soon the long gray days, the doldrums of the workbook, music lessons and arithmetic. Hours spent staring out the window at row upon row of stratus clouds stretching beyond the horizon, clouds that promise nothing except never to end, and waiting for the bell to ring.

The Learning Curve

There are certain concepts that I only vaguely understand but that people talk about all the time. You frequently hear the term "learning curve", for instance. I suppose that refers to how one learns a new skill or gains knowledge over a period of time, described as an ascending arc from zero (knowing nothing) to ten, the zenith (knowing all there is to know about a thing). Then comes the gradual descent, the arc of forgetting, back to zero. Then, feet firmly planted on the ground in the batting box of ignorance, the learning curve ball comes whistling past and slowly you come to understand that once again you are out.

Spring Again

Seagulls sailing close to the wind, clouds running before, everything moving, the waves breaking on some far shore and the water here, all rippled and nervous, the sun stirring the wind which has pushed the ice far out to sea. The sun itself comes spinning in from deep space, the snow melting, pussy willows and catkins, marsh marigolds in the ditch, leaves turning green again, everything wanting and growing. It seems to indicate… something. But what? Was Aunt Ruth Uncle Karl's sister? What happened to the farm? There is no one to ask. No one and nothing has any more idea what's going on than you do. You are now the resident expert.

As Is

We've sold the house so we have to move. Now I don't have to think about cutting down that old ugly silver maple tree. I don't have to worry about the squirrels in the attic or mowing the lawn. Not my problem. I intend to blow away like the fluff from a dandelion. One of the last things I'll do before we leave is to drag the old Adirondack chair out to the street corner to be hauled away by anyone who wants it. Sinister device! Sit down there and you may never be able to get up again.

Supervisor

They have knocked down the old school, across the street, bulldozed the little woods nearly out of existence. They are putting up new shops and building affordable housing for students and seniors. All day the trucks and front-end loaders are at work filling the air with dust and noise. I sit and watch as if I were some kind of supervisor. People walk by and say, "How's it going?" "Great," I say. "Right on schedule."

A Man Builds a House

Once when I was in high school I had a temporary summer job cleaning up around a construction site. The house under construction belonged to a dentist and he was doing a lot of the work himself. Most of the time I was alone on the site but once a day the dentist would drive up in his white pickup truck to check on the progress. One day without even saying hello he said, "I had to divorce my wife the other day. I hated to do it but there wasn't any choice." He said it the way that a man would say he had to shoot his favorite dog. "Really?" I said. On another occasion he said, "You know if we have another war it will be with the English." "Really?" I said. "Yep," he said. "They have been our enemy since 1776. You can't trust those Brits, they want this country back." Then the day I finished up the job he came and paid me off. "Doctor says I've got cancer. I guess I'm going to die." He paused and looked around. "I just hope I can finish this house." I was 17, I didn't know what to say. I still don't.

The Ineffable

Most of my life I was not paying attention, I think. That's why I remember so little-- the names of lovers and intimate friends, forgotten, the houses I lived in, the kinds of cars I drove.... What was I thinking about, then? The ineffable, of course. I was trying to capture the ineffable. The way a person might set a live trap and catch a skunk. What now? It's a difficult situation. Certainly not the stay against confusion Frost talked about. I've heard a lot of skunk stories, and it seems to me that they all have unfortunate and ridiculous endings: baths in tomato juice and buried clothing. One story involved dynamite in the crawl space beneath a house. I believe that the person in the story was a great-uncle of mine.

Could

Words are very strange. If you look at word long enough it begins to seem odd. The word, jump, for instance. An odd word to my ear, but I suppose appropriate, juh for the effort of going up and ump for coming down to earth, and it all happens quickly: jump. Other words make less sense to me. "Honey, how do you spell could?" "Could? C-o-u-l-d, why do you ask that?" "Well, that's what I wrote but suddenly it didn't look right." It seems that c-o-u-l-d, should be pronounced cold or cooled But then should would be pronounced shooled and would would be wooled. Could shood be spelled c-o-o-d, like good. C-o-u-l-d doesn't look right. Could meaning the possibility exists. It could happen.

The Black Journal

In the black journal there are a number of entries about the weather and the slant of the winter light. There is an observation of how sea smoke rises from the cooling body of water, along with some unintelligible scribbling about form and substance. On page 21 there are a few ideas for financial reorganization. Then on page 23 some notes about ice fishing. After that there are many, many blank pages.

As the Light Turns Green

The faith of saints is absolute. There is order beyond all this dying, eating and begetting. Beyond the work week, in the fullness of time, reason will be made manifest. A saint is lifted as a solitary star into the firmament. One by one, as the light turns green, we mortals merge into the Great Flow but a saint will cross six lanes of traffic to reach the posited exit.

Saints

As soon as the snow melts the grass begins to grow. Even though the daytime high is barely above freezing, even though May is very like November, marsh marigolds bloom in the swamp and the popple trees produce a faint green that hangs under the low clouds like a haze over the valley. This is the way the saints live, no complaints, no suspicion, no surprise. If it rains carry an umbrella, if it's cold wear a jacket.

Nothing in Particular

Head bowed, hands folded I may look as if I am saying my prayers, and since I don't really believe in any religion you might say I am saying my prayers to nothing in particular. Or, to put a more positive spin on it, saying my prayers to everything in general, prayers to the chicken house, the freeway, the fading light and the dusty air. If you could see me sitting in my lawn chair on the back porch, it might appear that I have humbled myself before all the phenomena of the earth…or that I have dozed off again in the late afternoon sun.

Worldly Goods

I've sold or given away most of my books and my tools, and most of my fishing gear and my canoe. I have only one rod and reel left, so some days I sit and fish and some days I just sit. There is a certain satisfaction in the divesting of worldly goods, as there is in quitting a job, a kind of spiritual release, a sanctimony. And every day I feel that I become more Godlike, in that soon, like God, I won't do anything at all.

Complete Strangers

These days I find it hard to remember which of my contemporaries are dead and which are still alive. But to tell the truth when I meet them on the street or in the grocery store the dead ones don't look that much worse than the living, and none of them has much to say. Mostly, we have found it mutually advantageous to ignore one another, pretending not to see, or that we are complete strangers, and the years pass and eventually we forget entirely. But occasionally there may come one of those awkward moments, at a party or someplace, when our host says, "Art, have you met Elwin?" And there is one of my long dead acquaintances. "Oh, yes I say," shaking Elwin's hand, "we're old friends, we go back a long way." Then, sometime later I wonder, "Now, what was that guy's name?"

What We Mean When We Say It's a Beautiful Day

The summer was a disappointment, rain and cold wind. People say, "Last year summer was on a Tuesday, I think. I missed it because I had to work." The garden did not do well. Now it is fall, the leaves bright red, orange and gold in the sunshine, a beautiful day.

Someone says, "Isn't it a nice day?" "Beautiful!" is the proper response. That means the sun is shining, may be only 20 degrees and the north wind a bit sharp, nevertheless we will not be pushed around. It is a beautiful day.

It means the wind has shifted. It means the snow has stopped falling. It means melt water is running in the street. It means we are still alive. It means the sun is shining and it is a beautiful day.

Fidget

In my younger days when I had insomnia I would lie awake and worry about things, things in the past that were over, mistakes I had made that were too late to repair. Or I would worry about things to come, difficulties that might never happen. Nowadays I am simply awake, not much to plan for or worry about. So I roll over, scratch, yawn, turn over again, wiggle my toes. The hours go by and I fidget.

Soup

In the yard of her place on a branch of the Knife River, she mixed in the big cast iron pot, aspen bark, birch root, garlic and beets, spruce gum, willow twigs, water from the creek, (tasting slightly of crankcase oil) a moose joint, fish heads, cinnamon and wild ramps, mushrooms gathered by the light of the Hunter's Moon. She added onion and bitter herbs, a touch of sumac, red pepper, some withered apples that still clung to the tree, cabbage and gnarled potatoes. All day the smoke swirled through bare branches and the crows overhead circled and dived. When, at last, she took a taste with the big wooden spoon it wasn't right. Each ingredient should blend so that each taste was a reminiscence, sensibly tempered, a joy, a tonic against the ague and the grippe, against old age and the grinding cold winter. But it wasn't right this year, flat somehow. . . . It needed something. But what was it? She went over the recipe again because she forgot things more easily now. It wasn't right and anytime now the guests might arrive.

Small Things

Once you stood, brooding, on the cliff overlooking the turbulent sea and the tumultuous clouds, the wind blowing your long hair and the tails of your frock coat. Your role was to make as much noise as possible. Sturm und Drang. But what about the beautiful Marguerite? Ah, forget her... the world so vast....

Now your concerns have diminished somewhat. The seas continue to rise, the wind blows, the war goes on. You consider the wing of a bird, a stalk of grass, the late glimmer on the stream surface, realizing that this may be the last time you see any of these things again in this peculiar light. Small things. Like that sliver in the very tip of your finger that despite your best efforts resists removal, so small it is almost invisible, yet when you touch anything, it hurts.

Hidden Meanings

Once I thought that things had meanings, that perhaps the river flowing, the wind moving a maple branch was a kind of secret signal being sent, a signal, a meaning that always just eluded me. It seemed that if I spread my arms that same wind could carry me into the sky. Now that I am old I happily realize that things and incidents, the bright red leaves tossing in the wind, beautiful as ever on the hillside, the secret world, has no meanings to impart, no hidden messages. But that too, eludes me.

Yellow Hat

Nobody knows what will happen, what catastrophes, what miraculous transformations. In order to maintain faith, to plan for the future, the world must be simplified. Here is the window out of which you can see a tree, a bright red flower, green grass extending over the hill. On top of the hill, yes, there I am... two legs, two arms, ten fingers like sausages and a smile on my big round face. And just six inches above my yellow hat the blue sky begins.

About Louis Jenkins

Louis Jenkins was born and raised in Oklahoma. In 1971, he moved with his wife Ann to Duluth, Minnesota where he lived for 45 years and spent most of that time complaining about the weather. His poems have been published in a number of literary magazines and anthologies. He has published 17 collections of his poetry. Mr. Jenkins was awarded two Bush Foundation Fellowships for poetry, a Loft-McKnight fellowship, and was the 2000 George Morrison Award winner. Louis Jenkins has read his poetry on A Prairie Home Companion and was a featured poet at the Geraldine R. Dodge Poetry Festival in 1996 and at the Aldeburgh Poetry Festival, Aldeburgh, England in 2007. Beginning in 2008, Louis Jenkins and Mark Rylance, Academy Award winning actor and former director of the Globe Theatre, London, began work on a stage production titled *Nice Fish*, based on Mr. Jenkins poems. The play premiered April 6, 2013 at the Guthrie Theater in Minneapolis and ran through May 18, 2013. A revised version of the play was performed at American Repertory Theater in Boston (Jan.-Feb 2016) where, thanks to Mark Rylance and Claire Van Kampen, Mr. Jenkins got a chance to attempt acting. It was a short-lived career. The play then moved to St. Ann's Warehouse in New York City (Feb.-March 2016). In November 2016 the play opened at The Harold Pinter Theatre in London's West End, and ran until February 12, 2017. In March 2017 Nice Fish was nominated for an Olivier award, Best new comedy, 2017.